ZEN
For Beginners!

The Ultimate Zen Guide To a Happier, Simpler, More Fulfilling Buddhist-Inspired Lifestyle

By Dominique Francon

Table of Contents

Conclusion: Breathe Out - Keep Calm And Breathe On

Preview Of "Buddhism For Beginners! - The Ultimate Guide To Incorporate Buddhism Into Your Life – A Buddhism Approach For More Energy, Focus, And Inner Peace"

About the Author

Disclaimer

The information provided in this book is designed to provide helpful information on the subjects discussed. The author's books are only meant to provide the reader with the basics knowledge of the topic in question, without any warranties regarding whether the reader will, or will not, be able to incorporate and apply all the information provided. Although the writer will make his best effort share her insights, the topic in question is a complex one, and each person needs a different timeframe to fully incorporate new information. Neither this book, nor any of the author's books constitute a promise that the reader will learn anything within a certain timeframe.

Dedicated to those who love going beyond their own frontiers.

Keep on pushing,

Dominique Francon

Introduction
Breathe In - What Zen Buddhism Teaches Us

Thank you for taking the time to start reading this book. No, really. Honestly—*thank you*. I know how much trouble it is these days to actually buy a book (even a lowly eBook!), proverbially flip it open and actually read it. It's a rarity. It's hard to find the time to sit down and just read something anymore. It used to be the norm, but now it's beyond in decline—it's frankly uncommon.

We're very busy these days.

It's been a busy month.

Busy year, actually.

Maybe an entire busy life.

Look, I get it. I'm a busy girl too. Just this week I've had to finish writing this eBook, contact my marketing team, update my blog, deal with the dozen other clients I write for, prepare my own lunches, cook my own dinners, exercise at least three times a week, keep friendly with my friends, and spend a bit of time with my family.

As an entrepreneur I have to keep active on Twitter and Facebook to promote my work; as an occasional freelance writer I have to manage strict deadlines that don't always work in my favor; as a friend I have to be there when my friends need me; as a family woman I need to, well, just see my family once in a while, which is an increasing rarity.

When do I read? I feel ashamed in admitting it, but it took my three months to finish the last book I read. I just started another one two weeks ago—I'm only on page 30. I've barely touched it this week, in fact.

We're all busy people. Our priorities are different—some are busy because they're taking care of sick relatives or working late hours to provide for their families. Teenagers are busy socializing and kids are busy playing. Mothers are busy cleaning and fathers are busy commuting.

What does all this business do to our minds?

It's eroding them, slowly but surely. Our brains are among the most complex systems of chemicals and neurons on this planet. No computer is more nuanced than our emotions, and no other creature capable of thinking logically or understanding concepts like faith, mathematics, envy, devotion or artistry. We are profoundly unique in this world, maybe even this universe. But when we corrupt our lives with nuisances and distractions—worrying over money, preoccupying ourselves with self-consciousness, concern over our body image, hating the religious beliefs of others, stressing over new technology—we're losing that core essence of what makes us human.

The more clutter we introduce into our lives, the more we distance ourselves from one another.

The more material goods invade our homes, the less human we become.

Buddhism is a 2,500-year-old philosophical belief born out of a mountainous region that is now the Nepalese Himalayas. At its core has always been spiritual peacefulness and meditative mindfulness—exactly the tools, I would argue, that we need most today. Except the problem is, Buddhism is actually an incredibly complex philosophy (I avoid calling it a "religion" because religion implies belief in a god or deity, which Buddhism negates—instead it promotes belief in the power of oneself), easily as complicated as Christianity, Islam or Judaism. There are strict rules and doctrines, thousands of years of written scripture and a bit of debatable mythology, like karmic rebirth and nirvana, that can seem hard to buy into for new students.

And none of this is to even begin mentioning its myriad regional and historical sects, including the main divisions, Mahayana and Theravada Buddhism, and beyond them offshoots like Pure Land, Nichiren, Cheontae and, of course, Zen.

Zen is an interesting one because it's so commonly simplified to meet our Western standards that it has really grown far from its roots in 6th century China. For instance, you were probably surprised I just wrote China and not Japan—when we think of Zen, we think of those raked sand Zen Gardens, blissful red wooden temples in Kyoto and Japanese karate masters whose minds are firm against the intrusions of the outside world.

All these stereotypical representations are sort of accurate, but only to a point. Zen is indeed of Chinese origin—and we'll go over that all in the next chapter, a brief history lesson—and what it stands for has more to do with consciously mastering your mind rather than just raking some sand and plopping down into it a few pebbles.

But right now I want to clarify one thing before we get started: to be Zen can be easy. If you really commit to it—and I mean truly let go of your fundamental habits, things you previously believed were absolutely necessary to your life, like cars and savings accounts and being in the know of upcoming tech and fashion trends—Zen can come you to naturally.

It's all about breathing, mindfulness and meditation. You need to first be aware of how your body works and how that affects your mind. You need to first understand the correlation between the physical and spirit worlds.

But don't get me wrong—I don't expect you to actually give up all these material goods. (If you gave up your iPad, how would you ever have found this book?) Rather, I want to help you keep your aesthetic life in check, and re-focus your energy on yourself as well as your surroundings. I want to help you from becoming too wrapped up in little details. I want to help you enjoy *your* life more, rather than replacing it with someone else's life.

So take a deep breath in. Hold it. Hold it. Hold it.

Okay, now release it.

Let's get started.

To truly understand Zen, we must first understand a bit about Buddhism.

Buddhism is a non-theist philosophy—there's no God, there's no Allah, and you don't actually pray to Buddha in temples the way we might think of praying to a Judeo-Christian God. The original Buddha was, in fact, a man named Siddhartha Gautama.

Gautama was a rich kid, born into royalty as a prince of a region of northeastern India near the Himalayas, which is today part of southern Nepal. From what records tell us, Gautama was an extremely bright kid—always inquisitive, always asking questions about the world—but his life of extreme comfort and luxury meant that he never had to receive any answers. He had no idea how the world really worked—he was naïve.

Gautama also realized, one day, in his teens or 20s, that he was not especially happy with his life. It wasn't just late teenage angst, either, although it might have been a bit of that—it was more that all the money in the world could not buy him the happiness and wisdom that he sought. He felt kind of empty inside.

When he was 29-years-old, Gautama left the palace grounds for the first time. He asked his accompanying guards what was wrong with these people he was seeing—why were they so miserable? What made them so skinny? Why are they suffering? Why aren't they happy? What's caused them to be so sick?

Naturally, it was a bummer to find out that the real world was not the aesthetic world of golden luxury that he'd been raised in.

Over the next six years, Gautama tore through every type of religious belief he could at the time. He became an ascetic student and stopped dressing in warm clothes and bathing. He gave up his material life and began instead begging for alms in the street to learn how to be humble.

Later he tried Hinduism, Taoism and yoga. He meditated alongside the brightest minds of his day. He learned patience and the power of inner peace and solitude, and impressed all of his teachers—so much so that they all invited him to stay and practice meditation full-time as a master of the system. But Gautama was never fully satisfied with any of these doctrines, and rejected every offer out of hand.

The last thing he tried was the most extreme: self-mortification. This means depriving oneself not just of all material luxuries, but also of basic needs like food and drink. He allegedly ate only a single leaf or nut every day, nearly starving himself to death. Lying down one day, incapacitated and depressed, a 10-year-old girl, Sujata, came up to him and offered him some rice milk. He was suddenly overwhelmed by her generosity and accepted the offer, ending his years of asceticism and beginning a new tactic of meditation.

So the story goes, he sat beneath the Bodhi Tree, which can today be found in Bodh Gaya, India, in the distant groves near the Neranjara riverbanks. He fell deep into a meditative trance, in which he stayed for 49 days without speaking, eating, drinking or moving. This is what's known as his Enlightenment.

Once he awoke, he became known as the Buddha—a title which actually just means "Awakened One" or "Enlightened One".

The original Gautama Buddha, by the way, looks like this:

So you might be wondering a few things, like what he did after he woke up, and who that big fat Buddha is that you see in all those Chinese restaurants.

Well, this is where Buddhism gets complicated. Really complicated. Buddha spread the word of Four Noble Truths, a key phrase in any Buddhist philosophy, and something we're going to touch on a lot in this book.

The Four Noble Truths, very quickly, are:

1. Suffering exists.
2. Every suffering has a cause.
3. Suffering can be ended.
4. How we can end our suffering.

They're deeper than that, of course, but the breakdown is that we as conscious humans are capable of controlling our own lives, and as a result mediating our own happiness.

This is at the core of Zen Buddhism, too, of course. Zen confirms that first we must acknowledge that suffering exists—in the world, there is starvation and crime, but also within ourselves there is doubt, pity and anger.

After we acknowledge it, we must understand its cause, which is often a craving for something, like power or respect. (I crave respect, so I act harsh towards my employees; I crave power, so I invade another country, and so forth.)

Once we understand the cause of our suffering, we must understand that it *can* end. We must remove ourselves from our problems as much as possible, and understand that petty emotions such as jealousy and hatred are not *who* we are, but feelings we draw into ourselves for a period of time before letting go of. The trick is to let go before they even set in.

Lastly, Buddha tries to teach us how we can end that suffering, which is itself a lengthy and often-studied series of life lessons known as the Eightfold Path. The Eightfold Path aims to direct us on the right path to a good, harmonious life, by teaching us the Right View, Right Thoughts, Right Speech, Right Action, Right Livelihood, Right Effort, Right Mindfulness and Right Meditation. This Eightfold Path to happiness seeps into every Buddhist sect in the world.

There's also a lot of stuff about karma (how you act now affects your future), rebirth (related to karma) and nirvana (if all goes well and you're truly enlightened, you stop being reborn and shoot straight up into nirvana, the Buddhist heaven). But those aren't as relevant to the Zen mindset, so we'll dodge around them for now.

What Makes Zen Different

So, now that we understand a bit of basic Buddhist history, what makes Zen special?

You have to understand, Buddhism didn't stay intact for very long. Only a few hundred years after the Buddha's death at age 80 (he ate a wild poisonous mushroom, the poor guy), his disciplines got into fights over the correct way to study his teachings—some of the monastic leaders claimed that there was a strict way to achieve enlightenment, and that way necessarily involved their structural system that adhered to Buddha Gautama's teachings. This is today known as Theravada Buddhism, and is considered the "purer" form of Buddhist insofar as it deals exclusively with the original texts. Today, Theravada Buddhism is most prominent across South and Southeast Asia: India, Sri Lanka, Myanmar, Nepal, Thailand, Laos and Cambodia.

The offshoot, led by peasants and common people upset at the elitism of the monastic leaders, became known as Mahayana Buddhism, which spread north and northeast to countries like Vietnam, China, Japan and Korea. The Mahayana Buddhists believed that anyone could achieve enlightenment—they sort of leveled the playing field. According to Mahayana Buddhism, there have been millions of Buddhas in the world, including that big fat guy you've seen in Chinese restaurants. (His name is Budai, by the way, and he existed in the 10th century in China, long after the original Buddha passed away. That's why you'll rarely see statues of jolly old Budai in Southeast Asian temples, which otherwise exclusively erect monuments to the original Buddha.)

Here's where Zen fits in: Because Mahayana Buddhism was so focused on everyday people being able to achieve enlightenment, eventually that concept developed even further, to the point that Buddhist scriptures take a backseat altogether and one's own mind is the most important. That's why in Zen temples you rarely see statues of any Buddha.

Zen Buddhism was introduced in China in the 6th century as Chan Buddhism by a monk named Bodhidharma. Bodhidharma is often conveyed as a hairy, angry-looking fellow with big bulging eyes and a wrinkly forehead. His biographical details are sketchy at best—some say he was South Indian, while Japanese lore has him hailing from Persia. He is generally depicted like this:

Bodhidharma is known as the father of Zen Buddhism, because he was the first to introduce the concept of enlightenment as a personal expression of direct insight into the teachings of the original Buddha, rather than focusing on the wording of the teachings themselves. Knowing all the sutras and adherence to the specific rules became less important than achieving what Buddha originally intended everyone to achieve—enlightenment. To that end, Bodhidharma's most famous act—and most controversially described, actually—was his nine-year-long stint of gazing straight ahead at a cave wall the ultimate form of meditative enlightenment.

It could be argued that Bodhidharma recognized that the world was different nearly a thousand years ago when the original Buddha existed, and that what technological and architectural ancements had been made changed the way people lived—Buddha's own life was, in a sense, biblical in its primitivism, so his specific instructions were less important than the themes he communicated. He emphasized the importance of *zazen*, a Zen form of meditation that demands clearing your mind of all things to achieve natural enlightenment.

Think of this whole thing like the evolution of Christianity, if that's a more familiar story: Catholicism was the predominant religion for years and years. According to Catholics, the Pope was the most important person in the world, church was where God lived and priests and bishops were necessary for salvation. Then along came Martin Luther and changed all that: in laying the groundwork for Protestantism, he destroyed the hierarchy of Catholicism and made the whole religion simply between individuals and God. Later still, churches like the United Church take that Protestant attitude one step further.

In this example, the hierarchical structure is Theravada Buddhism, the rebellious power-to-the-people Lutherans are Mahayana Buddhists and Zen is like the United Church of today. Except Zen is much, much stricter than the church in its proper form.

To be a proper Zen Buddhist, you need to join a monastery, shave your head every five days, meditate constantly and accept being whacked with a stick by the higher-up monks who see you moving even slightly. Zen Buddhists will spend all day digging holes in the ground, finding stones, cleaning them and doing nothing with them—it is work for the sake of work, to clean your mind of excess thoughts and hone on bodily actions. They chop a lot of wood, too—not for fires or building anything, but just for the sake of chopping wood. They accept eating modestly, sleeping only three or four hours each day and getting frostbite on their ears if it's cold outside.

True Zen Buddhism is harsh, but the results are palpable: people who've spent time in them report that their minds feel lighter, their bodies become lither, their worries ease away. They realize how they can, in fact, live without material wealth. They sleep on hard wooden floors and face the harsh elements without abandon.

Because Zen Buddhists traditionally demand their minds to be cleansed of any outer thoughts or infections, they confine themselves to strict lifestyles and material abstinence.

It is not like Theravada or Mahayana Buddhism, where meditation demands complete focus over your body and emotional control—in Zen, the key concept is *emptiness.* You have to clear your mind before you can do anything else.

Today, the Western world has adopted this to mean that Zen is all about simplicity—living with less, caring less about money, being truer to your own emotions and clearing your mind for meditative sessions. Let's be clear: Western Zen isn't truly authentic Zen by any means, but that doesn't mean we can't use the word to help us change our lifestyles for the better.

Now that we're on the same page, and we understand the distinctions between types of Buddhism and what Zen really is, let's start the real practical lessons: how adopting Zen habits can help you clean out your mind and live a fuller, happier life.

Chapter 2: The Key to Happiness Exists (HINT: It's Not What You Think)

Have you ever meditated before? Just sat down on a plush cushion, cleared away any and all thoughts, and focused simply on breathing—in, then out, then in, then out? And stayed there for 45 minutes?

I bet you haven't. I mean, jeez, even I haven't—not for 45 minutes. Real meditation is as much a skill as it is a tactic for healthy minds. Real meditation demands a level of patience, spare time and dedication that most of us don't bother with.

Why don't we bother? Well, that's easy: people generally don't do something when there isn't an immediate gain. Exercising is difficult because going for an hour-long run—even once a day for a full week—won't make you as thin as you want. We go to bed late because we'd rather stay up and be entertained by TV or social media, because, heck, seven hours from now we'll wake up again, and seven hours from now is much harder to plan for than the *now*.

Eating, on the other hand, brings immediate pleasure. TV makes us laugh *now*. Being drunk isn't something we do for posterity— we drink because we want to feel better in the present moment. Why wait? Living a hedonistic life is not only contagious—it's also just downright fun.

(Quickly, I want to address the contradiction here—that we live hedonistically in the now, but Zen Buddhism also teaches us that living in the present moment is more important than worrying about the future or regretting the past. This is true, and we're going to address the contradiction soon—because Zen teaches us to appreciate the present without distraction, in a purely mindful state, meaning no eating or binge drinking. But, again, more on that later.)

The point is that eating and drinking and watching TV are fun now, and meditation—along with hard work and exercise, which reap intangible rewards like "discipline" and "manners" and "health" that we can't taste or smell immediately—gets brushed aside. I cannot tell you the number of times I've put off cleaning my bed sheets because I can't feel the dirt on them. Why bother washing them? There's no reward in that for me, unless you really, really like the smell of clean linens, which I don't care for one way or the other.

The problem is that these benefits are hidden. We don't understand what meditation can do for us until we've tried it, and we'll never try it unless we know what it can do for us. It's a totally vicious cycle that results in, basically, never doing it. And worse still—there seems to be absolutely no repercussion, because we've never tried it so we don't know what we're missing. We just go on living our lives, existing in blissful distraction and emotional clutter.

So, okay. Let's try actually meditating. Just *once.* After all, the original Buddha Gautama once commanded people, if they wanted to achieve happiness, to "resolutely train yourself to achieve peace." Nobody said peace could be achieved easily, of course. It takes, as is quoted, resolute training.

So let's give meditation a shot, even if you feel silly doing it. And when we're done, let's see what happens, okay?

How Do I Even Do It?

If you're like most people, you might imagine that meditation goes something like this: you close your eyes, cross your legs awkwardly, connect your thumb to your ring finger, mumble "ohm…" and stay like that for 10 minutes.

It's not quite that, although you can do that if you want—Zen meditation is more than just that.

Some traditional meditation involves counting your breaths or chanting positive mantras to your friends, families and strangers. Zen Buddhists don't do that. The good-vibrations (dare I say "hippie"?) form of Western Buddhism is separate from the more relaxed, clear-conscience Zen method of meditation.

Zen meditation is called *zazen*, and is at the heart of the Zen philosophy—to the point that Zen is actually known Buddhism's "Meditation School".

Zazen allows us to sit down and observe life in a pure state, every day for a set amount of time. The meditation aims to combine our corporeal reality with our breathing and mental patterns. There is no distinction between any part of the self in *zazen*.

Here's how to do it.

First, you need a good physical position, because the position of our bodies suggests how our mental states exist. If we slump, we feel worthless. If we flex, we feel strong. Therefore, with *zazen*, we aim to replicate the original meditative position heralded by Buddha Gautama 2,500 years ago: a stable sitting position in perfect symmetry. We ground ourselves on the floor to avoid shaking or movement of any sort. There's also something called a *zafu*, a small cushion, underneath our butts so that our knees, in a cross-legged stance, can touch the ground for even more stability.

There are a number of specific positions—Burmese, Half-Lotus, Full-Lotus, Seiza or Chair—which we won't get into specifically here, because you can look up the differences online. It's mostly a matter of what feels more comfortable for you. The important thing is that, regardless of your personal stance, your back remains straight and your body remains grounded and secure. You want as little movement as possible so that you can focus your mind on what matters. A straight back also is better for our diaphragms to allow deep breaths in and out.

The idea is that we do as little as possible to affect change. Don't wear tight clothes or anything uncomfortable. Breathing should happen normally—you shouldn't even have to think about it, it should just happen automatically, as breathing does.

Zazen meditators tend to suggest nasal breathing instead of mouth breathing. Swallow naturally. Keep your eyes lowered and all but close them so you don't have to blink repeatedly. Relax your muscles and tuck in your chin so your neck doesn't ache.

The idea behind all of this is to minimize yourself as much as possible, and to remove all the aspects of life that clutter our daily lives—even the tiniest things, like breathing and blinking.

Next, hand position is key. None of that hands-on-knees stuff you might see elsewhere—*zazen* is all about what's called the "cosmic mudra". It should resemble a gentle circle with your palms facing up around the groin area. Using your dominant hand (which for most of us is the right), hold your opposite hand in the palm-up position in a cupping position. Touch your thumbs gently. It should look like this:

The reason is to focus your energies downward. This is also why your eyes should be downcast. Above, there are distractions, like clouds or ceiling fans. Below there is only the grounded earth. Our hands should be near what in Zen is known as the *hara*—our anatomical centers, a few inches just below our bellybuttons. It is considered the spiritual and emotional center of our bodies, and we should direct all our energies there.

Next is the most important factor: breathing. On every Zen website, with every Zen master, breathing will be the number-one focused on aspect of meditation. Breath and air are vital life forces. Zen masters teach us that our breathing is inextricably linked to our thoughts—when we're anxious, we breathe anxiously; when we're calm, we breathe slowly. When so-called magicians submerge themselves underwater for over 15 minutes, their greatest skill is not being worried—worry causes faster breathing. They need to suppress their natural anxieties and be completely at peace, breathing as slowly as possible for much longer than we are normally used to.

Then we need to find our center of gravity. This involves a bit of rocking back and forth in gentle increments, in decreasing arcs, until we are comfortable in a single sitting position.

From that point on, it's all in the breathing. Begin with a counting technique—count up to ten for every inhalation and every exhalation, and let the numbers be the sole and exclusive thoughts that occupy your mind. Go like this:

Inhale, one.

Exhale, two.

Inhale, three...

And so on, like that, until you count all the way up to ten. Then, guess what? You just start over again. The goal here is a trick: the goal is that there *is* no goal. Like the Zen monks who chop wood for days on end, or the students who dig holes just to clean rocks for no purpose, the idea is to stabilize your mind and rid yourself of clutter. While those are physical duties, meditation is the mental one.

If you start to think about other things—what your friends are up to, or what you're going to cook for dinner—acknowledge the thought and let it go. You want to actively kick out every excess thought you can.

With enough practice, you will be able to stop counting altogether and focus simply on breathing. You want to reintroduce breathing to your life—remind yourself how it should come naturally and without focus. Once you've accomplished that, you can fully cleanse your mind of extra junk and experience what Zen Buddhists understand as a healthier, cleaner lifestyle.

A few words of warning: this won't come quickly or easily. Some pop Western Zen teachers advise that interested students start with just two minutes a day—but two minutes *every* day, without exception—and to only bump it up once you feel comfortable to three, four, six, eight, 15 minutes, until you're at a point where you feel you can comfortably control yourself in the *zazen* position.

Also, know that sometimes you will become distracted by thoughts, especially during important stages of your life—if you have a job interview, or your girlfriend just broke up with you, or something like that. Don't use meditation as an excuse to avoid important life decisions. You may find that the thought will interrupt your meditative process constantly, and you will be unable to focus. Don't worry—that's natural. It's not a failure so much as a hint that you should solve this problem first. That's part of what *zazen* teaches us—it makes us aware of what's important in life, when we're confused by a daze of information and thoughts. It should distill out the most important parts of our lives.

If this chapter seemed abnormally long, I apologize. It's just that Zen meditation is at the core to Zen philosophy—it is like saying you should go to church if you want to be Catholic. Without it, there is no Zen philosophy at all.

So if you want to get started with Zen habits, the first thing to do is stop stressing and start relaxing. The way to do this is by *zazen*.

Even if it's just two minutes at first, close your eyes, take a few deep breaths, and focus on yourself. Take this time out every day and direct all your attentions on yourself, your body, your thoughts and—most importantly—your breathing. Even if you don't have time or the space to create the proper atmosphere, at least try to maintain a consistent style of at-home or at-work meditation. You'll find that it helps you calm down during stressful times, it will help you live simpler and slower, it will help you exercise mental control and memory, and it can help rein in a staccato heartbeat.

In fact, why don't you go ahead an try it right now. Two minutes. Go for it. When you're done, the next chapter will still be here, waiting for you.

In 1986, an Italian man named Carlo Petrini heard that McDonald's wanted to open a fast food chain restaurant near the beautifully preserved Spanish Steps in Rome. Petrini was furious. He was passionate about not only good food (he is, after all, Italian), but the culture that food brought with it—family dinners; relationships with your local farmer, butcher and fisherman; spending quality time by yourself or with others, cooking and cleaning the kitchen, rather than rushing from one appointment to another with a burger on the way. In his words:

> *"Today hardly anyone buys their wine directly from their trusted wine maker, or goes to the farm to buy eggs and a chicken or a rabbit; hardly anybody knows the baker who makes their bread, the charcutier who slaughters the pigs and cures the meat, the man who churns the milk of his sheep or goats to make cheese."*

This McDonald's, infesting the beautiful bastion of Roman life, was the last straw form him. He singlehandedly founded the Slow Food movement, a movement that sought to end reliance on fast food cravings and the desire to always rush everywhere, and instead revitalize the promotion of slow-cooked, home-grown meals. Petrini wants everyone to know where their ingredients come from. In this sense, Slow Food also refers to Fair Food, which involves a whole host of ethical debates surrounding food that we don't have time for here—instead, I'd like to point out one more quote by Petrini, taken out of the Slow Food Manifesto he helped pen in Paris in 1989:

> *"We need to choose the defense of tranquil material pleasure. Against those, and there are many of them, who confuse efficiency with frenzy, we propose the vaccine of a*

sufficient portion of assured sensual pleasure, to be practiced in slow and prolonged enjoyment."

Translation: slow down, everyone, and try enjoying your food for once.

The movement caught on, and today is prominent in over 150 countries, including virtually everywhere in the Western and developed worlds. The movement has official offices in Switzerland, Germany, New York City, France, Japan, the UK and Chile, and in 2004, Petrini helped found the University of Gastronomic Sciences, aimed at promoting healthy and nutritious cooking.

Okay. So what's the big deal? Some Europeans who care about food want everyone to enjoy the hours they took to make a meal, right? Why not—if it's cheaper—just indulge in a Big Mac now and again? What if I don't care that some farmers are struggling more now than they were a few centuries ago?

The thing is, this isn't an isolated instance of a Slow Movement, and farmers aren't the ones being hurt the most—you are, dear reader and eater of fast food. The more we indulge in frantic eating, the more we are admitting that we are busy, preoccupied people with scarcely enough time to eat a sandwich. By indulging in fast food, we are admitting that we need our food *fast*—as a society, as well as individuals.

The Slow Food movement caught on, by the way. The Slow Movement has evolved into Slow Media, Slow Art, Slow Design, Slow Science, Slow Cities and, simply, Slow Living—not to mention the dozens more Slow methods of working and living. People across the world are reacting to kinetic traffic and financial anxieties by simply slowing down their lives. This is not a food thing—this is a global lifestyle thing.

Slow Fashion promotes sustainable, ethically produced fashion garments. Slow Church is a conversation about how to slow down to let God into churchgoers' lives more meaningfully. Slow Gardening teachers outdoor lovers to enjoy the smells and sensations of gardening, rather than hurrying with a landscaper to achieve quick results. Slow Money investors are trying to steer market capital away from stock markets and hedge funds, and instead towards local farmers and start-up enterprises. Slow Travel aims to destroy the old tourist model of "fly in, see everything, stay in the hotel and leave" and replace it with spending more quality time in a single place to really absorb the atmosphere.

The common denominator here? Slow down to enjoy life. It's that basic. That's what Zen teaches us, too—to slow down, breathe in and out, meditate, think about life and regain control of ourselves.

Most people forget what's really important in life, but the Slow Movement is proof that it's not forgotten by everyone. While most of us may feel burdened with taxes and mortgages and the price of gas and raising good children and spousal fights, we forget how to prioritize. We forget that we can do all that stuff—take care of our kids and husbands and taxes—and still slow down. We needn't rush into everything.

Rushing is a direct result of feeling pressured to do something. This, I believe, is a result of envy. The tenth commandment (if we want to cross over from Zen to Judeo-Christian law for a moment) says to not covet thy neighbor's wife, house or life.

God may have been onto something that Buddha would agree with. Jealousy breeds pettiness and the feeling to surpass other people. When we see our neighbors with a new car, we wonder what we did wrong to not deserve one, too. When someone overtakes us on the highway, we get angry and want to drive faster.

I believe we all suffer from an innate fear of being left behind and forgotten.

Well, guess what?

You *will* be forgotten one day.

Not what you were expecting, is it? Maybe you want to be told that we're all special and unique snowflakes, all worth love and devotion and can achieve our dreams if we work hard? Well, maybe we can. But we've been brainwashed by conventional society into believing that that's the *only* way to live.

We live every day afraid of death—"I can't die yet," we might say. "I haven't accomplished enough yet."

If you believe that, you've been wasting your life. Instead of saying that, you should be able to—stick with me, here, morbid as it sounds—die at any moment and say, "I've lived a good life." If you spent all your life unhappy, with the hopes of attaining future happiness, what are you waiting for? Why waste the present moment when you could be enjoying it?

A core tenement of every type of Buddhism, but especially the Zen school, is that only the present moment exists—so savor it. That's why Zen students chop wood mercilessly, or clean stones to no end. It is to teach them that only their present actions matter, and not to worry about the past or future. The past and future do not exist, and never will exist. There is only the present. So slow down and enjoy it.

Now, to end this chapter, I'd like to address the contradiction I mentioned in the beginning of the last chapter on meditation. I mentioned that we're all too busy watching TV for immediate laughs and downing shots of vodka to have a good night to realize the effects of our actions in the future, and that investing in meditation is good for our future selves. But in this chapter, I realize, I wrote that we're all too focused on the future and should focus instead on the present.

I realize this sounds like a contradiction. It isn't. I don't consider watching TV to be "living in the present moment"—watching TV is a distraction that removes us from ourselves and places us outside our bodies, controls our minds and absorbs them into the story of the characters onscreen. There's no harm in a little distraction now and again, but too much is unhealthy.

Drinking and eating quickly, also, are not living in the present moment. Let's say you're eating a Big Mac. It's fast food. How can you be living in the moment when your only goal out of this meal is to eat quickly and get out of there? If your goal wasn't to eat quickly, why did you walk into a fast food restaurant? To savor every French fry? Come on. They're not that good.

Meditation shouldn't be seen as planning for your future, but it is—it is only because we can't yet fully appreciate its value. You need to trust me and other Zen practitioners when we say it's worthwhile. You need to put a little faith in the system, which, yes, is like investing in the future instead of living in the present. Except that meditation is the Zen *definition* of living in the present. We're not asking you to meditate in order to become a healthier person—what we're saying is you should meditate in order to appreciate your life more *right now*, and in the future, you'll find yourself a healthier person as a result.

The future goal is not the real goal. There are no real goals. There is no real future. Everything you do, you should do because it's the right thing to do in this very moment—take time to enjoy a good meal, feel your muscles stretch in a yoga position, listen to the sound of your breathing in a *zazen* stance.

In short: don't meditate for your future self. Meditate for your present self, and your future self will be happier when *his or her* present moment comes along.

Chapter 4: Get Rid of Excess Clutter, You DON'T Need It!

Louis C.K., for those unfamiliar, is a fiery-haired, large-gutted stand-up comedian from Boston. He's been called a "comic's comic" because his fame came slowly, well over a decade, and because he has a true gift for describing the world in ruthlessly clear terms without compromising his style to conform to the style of pop-comedians who occupy the mainstream stage.

Once Louis did an interview on Conan O'Brien's show in September, 2013. He began talking about why he didn't want his kids having smartphones.

I apologize for the following enormous blocks of text, but it's a brilliant story and I wanted to convey the fullest amount possible. Here's how he tells it:

> *"You need to build an ability to just be yourself and not be doing something. That's what the phones are taking away, is the ability to just sit there, like this... That's being a person, right? Because underneath everything in your life, there's that thing, that empty—"forever empty". You know what I'm talking about? ... It's down there. And sometimes when things clear away, you're not watching anything, you're in your car, and you start going, 'Ohhh no... Here it comes—that I'm alone!' That it starts to visit on you, just this sadness. Life is tremendously sad, just by being in it. That's why we text and drive. I look around, pretty much 100 percent of people driving are texting. And they're killing—everybody's murdering each other with their cars! But people are willing to risk taking a life and ruining their own cause they don't want to be alone for a second...*

"So anyway, I started to get that sad feeling and I started reaching for my phone and I said, you know what? Don't. Just be sad. Just let the sadness—stand in the way of it and let it hit you like a truck... And I let it come, and I started to feel, 'Oh my God'... And I pulled over and I just cried like a bitch, I cried so much. And it was beautiful. It was like this beautiful... Sadness is poetic. You're lucky to live sad moments. And then I had happy feelings because of it. Cause when you let yourself feel sad, your body has like antibodies, it has happiness that comes rushing in to meet the sadness. So I was grateful to feel sad—and then I met it with true, profound happiness. It was such a trip, you know? And the thing is, because we don't want that first bit of sad, we push it away with, like, a little phone or jacking off or some food, and you get a little... you never feel completely sad or completely happy. You just kinda satisfied with your product. And then you die."

This is a brilliant modern-day treatise on the degradation of our minds. And can you believe it—the entire time Louis was telling the story, people were in *hysterics*. They thought it was a funny bit. And it *was* funny, sure—Louis's an incredibly funny and talented man. But, like all the best comedians, he's also wiser than he lets on, and it's not until re-reading this bit—this mostly improvised bit of conversational interview with Conan O'Brien—that we can possibly appreciate its value.

The notion of pulling over in a car to just give in to an outpour of emotions is unheard of in our times. We're far too busy for that—and besides, it's *weird*, right? Why bother crying when we can simply suppress it, like he says, with a game of Candy Crush or a text message to a friend? And that line at the end: "You never feel completely sad or completely happy." When was the last time we felt true elation? Why not give into our emotions more often? Why not allow ourselves to exist in a more pure state? Why do we contort our own lives to fill somebody else's idea of happiness?

The answer, in part, is that we're too distracted. We distract ourselves constantly—with movies and TV, video games and books, homework and housework. We distract ourselves with culture because culture is so much more fun than real life.

An example: have you ever tried to exercise, and you put on the same type of music you once heard in a training montage? I'll use a dumb example I hope nobody out there has ever *actually* done: "Eye of the Tiger", from *Rocky.* In *Rocky*, Sylvester Stallone starts to beef up; he does push-ups, goes for runs up government steps, drinks raw egg yolks and the whole thing is over in two minutes. By the time it's done, he's in shape and happy about it.

You go for a run, put on "Eye of the Tiger", feel for a brief moment that you're Rocky in the movie—and then you actually have to *run for 30 minutes.* It's awful. Where's the fade to black? Where's the montage?

Culture has taught us that movie lives are easier to believe in than real lives. In romantic comedies, the handsome and beautiful leads almost always wind up together. In comedies, no matter how absurd the situation, the lead characters always turn out all right. In historical dramas, we always know the ending.

In real life, it's not so easy.

Zen Buddhism teaches us to live simpler lives, free of clutter and distraction. Zen monasteries are hidden away in the forested mountains of Japan, China and Korea. Monks live extremely sparse lives to remove all material wealth from themselves—they wear only robes, they shave their heads, they go for brisk pre-dawn hikes and eat mostly rice. It's hard to get further away from materialism.

Obviously nobody reading this book is going to do all that stuff, but we can still meet the monks partway, no? When we dematerialize our lives, we are admitting to ourselves the real world in which we live. We are facing reality headfirst and not distracting ourselves with smartphones or excess goods. We're saving time to enjoy quality meals, vacation time and our children and families.

Here are a few major lifestyle tips for lessening the impact of materialism in your life, so you can get rid of all that shit that doesn't matter and focus on what actually does.

First off, literally do the above—get rid of all that shit in your closet and basement. Donate old clothes and toys. You surely don't wear as many clothes as you actually own, yet every day, I bet you stare in the closet and wonder what to wear. Aside from the once or twice a year you wear that *one* shirt (you know the one), you see it every day and never wear it. Get it out of there. As for toys or souvenirs? Unless they're on display for legitimate aesthetic reasons, they're clutter. Throw them out. Give them away. Honestly, spending a weekend to clean up your house will work wonders to clearing the rest of your mind.

You should also limit the time you consciously waste window-shopping or staring at ads. Very rarely when we buy clothes do we actually need them, and this is a direct byproduct of being bored in a shopping mall. But maybe I'm harping on clothes too much— what about those As-Seen-On-TV ads? The more time you spend online, in front of the TV or looking at advertisements, the more aware you are of the material world. Our goal here is literally to *block it out* as much as possible. Don't even acknowledge that these items exist. You don't need them. Save yourself the time and money to invest in more important things.

Lastly, you should *strongly* mediate your social media time. Reddit, Pinterest and Twitter are all often awfully useless time-sucks that don't actually contribute to your wellbeing at all. You gain nothing from them. It's called *killing time* for a reason. Facebook is fine for communicative reasons, but use it strictly as a tool—that's what social media is, a tool for communication, not a lifestyle investment. Once we get too mired in the bog that is our online representations, we become obnoxiously self-conscious and begin to focus on all the wrong areas of our lives. We should be okay with being dislocated and disconnected. We'll deal with this theme more in the final chapter.

There are other things you can do, too, of course, in order to reduce your reliance on material goods. But ultimately, you know what's useful and what's necessary in your life. If you work in marketing, I can't very well justifiably tell you to get off Facebook. But you know as well as I do that you can spend less time lumbering around on it.

Even if meditation doesn't work for you, try going for walks more often. Clear your mind. Ease your anxieties. Actively try to *do less*. You'll find that once you've blocked our the unnecessary tidbits from your life, you'll have a lot more room to focus on the things that matter—yourself, your family and your friends.

Chapter 5: Why Only By Accepting Everything Can We Lose Nothing

How often did you say *"no"* yesterday? I'm going to go out on a limb and guess the answer was a lot.

A large part of our lives has become saying no to things. We are discerning creatures with limited time—sorry, I don't have time to listen to your sales pitch, I'm in the middle of dinner; sorry, I can't donate right now; no thanks, I'm super-busy, let's get lunch next week though, okay?

And then next week never comes, and no donations are made, and you live in a materialistically closed-off bubble for the rest of your life.

In 2005, British comedian Danny Wallace wrote a book—maybe you've heard of it—called "Yes Man". Danny vowed to never say "no" for an entire year, and spent that year with the wildest people, doing stunts he never before thought he could, and traveling the world. All he did was say, repeatedly, "Yes." The most famous quote from that book?

> *"Probably some of the best things that have ever happened to you in life, happened because you said yes to something. Otherwise things just sort of stay the same."*

It was later made into a kind of silly movie with Jim Carrey, but the intention was good. The intention as to prove that we can all become better people, just a little bit, if we stay a little more positive. The less we say "no", the less we negate from life; the more we say "yes", the more we accept in.

How is this a Zen philosophy, then? Zen Buddhism teaches early on that the universe is random. It's almost scientific in that way—

there is a good and proper way to live, and moral objectivity does exist, but the world does not act according to it. Zen, in this way, reflects very similarly against existentialism: we create our own lives ourselves, without reliance on outside deities or hidden miracles. We must focus entirely on ourselves and the power within our souls.

In this way, we have the power to make our lives better—we can't wait for someone else to come along and do it.

All the techniques I've been describing so far have led to this conclusion. Meditation? That's bringing yourself more in tune with your personal power and self-discipline. Slowing down? That's taking the time to appreciate what you have, because no one else can appreciate it for you. And dematerializing? That's clearing away all the useless junk so you can more firmly achieve your goals.

These are, in short, active steps you can take to make your life tighter and more coherent. But it also depends on doing it yourself.

Oftentimes in life we'll come across something we wish were different. Drivers will drive too slowly, or movie times won't coincide with our evening schedule, or people just don't do what we want them to do. In our ego-centric universes, this can be a major affront to our personal happiness.

In short: move at my speed or I'll be pissed off.

The answer, then, is to accept what we cannot change. (Which is *way* easier said than done, I know, but we're going to try to manage a new outlook together.) As Buddha Gautama once said, "People with opinions just go around bothering each other."

Before we step out into the world, we need to first acknowledge—say it aloud if you have to—that the world is an indifferent place. It is separate from your wills and wishes. You cannot control it, and you never will. All we do, as the old saying goes, is pay taxes and die.

Leo Babauta runs a fairly popular blog called Zen Habits. It's a good resource if you want years' worth of detailed posts on the subject of Western Zen lifestyles. Once, a few years ago, he wrote a post called "A Beautiful Method to Find Piece of Mind". In it, he wrote the following, frankly surprisingly candid note:

> "Expect things to go wrong, expect things to be different than we hoped or planned, expect the unexpected to happen. And accept it."

He then relates a story where he told his children, on a recent trip to Japan, to expect that things will go wrong. He prepped them for this, of course, telling them that it was all "part of the adventure". They understood, and when things went wrong (as they invariably do on trips to the ever-complicated Japan), and the Babautas missed a train and got rained out of Disney Sea and spent an hour commuting to a kids' theme park just to discover it was closed, Babauta writes that the kids were okay with it. They expected things to go wrong, and that's what happened.

I can't verify that these kids didn't scream in protest and that Babauta had to calm them down with ice cream or something—I don't know. But it's possible that they genuinely weren't bothered by the snags in the itinerary and were happy just to be adventurous.

It's a good mindset nonetheless: Babauta describes it as seeing the glass neither half empty nor half full, but as "already broken". That way, if it does break, you're prepared. The world is neither good nor bad—simply indifferent to your needs. Sometimes you get lucky, sometimes you don't. Accept it either way. That's Zen.

Later on, Babauta was inundated with replies calling him pessimistic and negative. Because he told people to expect to be let down, people felt let down by him. (I sincerely hope the irony was not lost on Babauta or any of his readers.)

Babauta then clarified his position: it's only negative if you see it as negative. He advised his readers to accept the world as it is, to accept his blog post as, amorally, a blog post, and not throw morality on top of it. Embrace what exists for what it is and stop trying to confirm the world to fit your ideals.

Remember the old Serenity Prayer goes, written by Reinhold Niebuhr and adopted by Alcoholics Anonymous:

> *"God, grand me the serenity to accept the things I cannot change, the courage to change the things I can, and the wisdom to know the difference."*

Know what you can change from what you can't, and you'll live a happier, more peaceful life. This view is not pessimistic—it is pragmatic. It acknowledges that the world is a difficult and complicated place to live in. The more you view the world as a harsh and unforgiving, the more defeated you will feel. The more you view the world as friendly and safe, the more naïve you will be.

See it as it really is. Don't kid yourself or others. Don't judge other people based on standards you invented—accept them for who they are.

And besides, who knows? Maybe one day something unexpected will happen: you'll be pleasantly surprised. If nothing goes wrong, consider yourself lucky, smile and carry on.

In January 2009, William Deresiewicz wrote an exceptionally shrewd and critical essay entitled "The End of Solitude" for the *Chronicle of Higher Education*. Google it. It's a terrific read.

In the absence of being able to legally copy and paste the whole thing here, I'm going to summarize a few key points. He essentially points out that we've lost our ability to enjoy solitude at all: that humans were once accustomed to solitude, in fact *relied* on it to appreciate the presence of God (through silent prayer); and, in the 18th and 19th century Romantic period, how poets replaced clergymen as distillers of this solitary beauty by rushing into cabins alone to write and contemplate life; then how, in the harsh light of modernity, solitude was seen as an affront to ourselves and our individuality, as communism and global corporations began to spring forth individualism that specifically required socialism (both politically and figuratively, as in simply being social) in order to thrive.

Then, in the mid-20th century, we witnessed suburbanization, intense physical isolation and a reliance on mass media like TV, radio and telephones to keep us connected. People became frantic at the prospect of being alone all of a sudden, and the internet—conveniently timed as it was—came to the rescue of lonely gay teenagers and idle mothers across America who wished to meet someone else like them.

Of course, this became too much of a good thing. "The contemporary terror is anonymity," as Deresiewicz writes, and he continues:

> *"The goal now, it seems, is simply to become known, to turn oneself into a sort of miniature celebrity. How many friends do I have on Facebook? How many people are reading my blog? How many Google hits does my name*

generate? Visibility secures our self-esteem, becoming a substitute, twice removed, for genuine connection. Not long ago, it was easy to feel lonely. Now, it is impossible to be alone."

And then, the *coup de grace*:

> *"Loneliness is not the absence of company, it is grief over that absence."*

Think about that for a second. That's really profoundly said.

I don't think that Deresiewicz is a Zen Buddhist, but it wouldn't surprise me too much if he were. His essay cuts to the heart of a major flaw in contemporary society—that we are terrified of being alone. It's exactly what Louis C.K. was saying earlier about cell phones and sadness. We have evolved to become afraid of being alone, because being alone means nobody cares, and we're all just a collection of fragile egos.

The easy trick is to gain a bit of self-esteem, and to become aware that your life has value—that your happiness matters—regardless of whether anyone else knows about it.

Let me repeat that: *Your happiness matters regardless of who knows it.*

Once you begin to focus too much on how much everyone else knows about you ("Just sun tanning at the beach!", you write on Twitter) rather than your own actual happiness (say, simply sun tanning at the beach and *not* tweeting it), then you're beginning to deconstruct your own life and create a life geared towards someone else.

Remember what we said in the last chapter: the world is an indifferent place. I'm not saying nobody else cares that much about your beach activities, but nobody should care as much as you. And you need to start enjoying your own present moment, instead of relying on others' approval to enjoy it.

Do you think I'm sounding too extreme? So what if you're tweeting at the beach? It's not a *reliance* on others to enjoy yourself, right? You can still enjoy it without tweeting about it.

Well, let's look at what happens when this approval disappears, but you still put yourself out there. Would you not be depressed if you posted on Facebook, to over 1,000 friends, that you were tanning on the beach and *nobody said a thing*? It would be like they're ignoring you.

And later, you post something else—about studying for an exam, or buying bundles of toilet paper on sale. And still, nobody "likes" it, nobody comments. Would you not feel a little hurt? Would you not start to wonder why you should even bother?

That's allowing the approval of others affect your happiness. The fact is, we need to revert to a time when we could act on our own volition to enjoy life and freely go about day-to-day activities without feeling pressured to live up to outside expectations.

In short, we need to learn to be alone.

Hobbies are a great way to be alone—knitting, cooking, building model airplanes, whatever. Some people write; others take photos. Try indulging in something that only you do. Give yourself some quality alone time.

Obviously, the Zen masters would prefer you spend this alone time meditating. But if you're too antsy for meditation, or you find it difficult to do that for more than two minutes per day, you should at least give yourself *something* to do by yourself.

As Deresiewicz notes, indulging in solitude requires "a willingness to be unpopular". That doesn't mean you should strive to shun your friends at every turn. But it does mean that you should have at least a few secrets that your friends don't know about—little things that make you happy that don't matter to others.

Create some time for yourself every day to indulge in a little solitude. This might mean, at a minimum, having a creative outlet or spending some time reading. Or else, if you want to simply lie in bed and listen to music, thinking about day-to-day problems and building up personal strength.

At an extreme, you might want to consider going on a trip by yourself. Take a weekend away. Go camping. Or, if you're less adventurous, go to the movies by yourself. (Why there's a stigma against seeing a movie alone, I'll never understand.)

As Henry David Thoreau once wrote, "I never found a companion that was so companionable as solitude. We are for the most part more lonely when we go abroad among men than when we stay in our chambers."

Once you indulge your solitude a little more, you'll learn something very important to the Zen lifestyle: being alone and being lonely are not the same thing. We can be alone without being lonely. And, in fact, we should be. It would do us great mental health if we spent more time to ourselves. We can, if nothing else, confront this painfully awkward fear of being alone that social media has instilled in us, and prove to the world that, yes, actually, we can live happier, more fulfilling lives while just breathing in and out, taking things one day at a time.

Chapter 7
Meditation Tips to Get Started - How to Sit & How Long Each Session Should Last (With Pictures!)

When it comes to meditation, there are some helpful tips you can follow to help ensure you'll get all of the benefits possible out of your sessions. Keep in mind that these are general tips, so you can pretty much play with them. The important thing to remember is that these tips and guidelines are meant to help guide you in hopefully obtaining a more mindful and focused meditation session. Breathing technique, posture, focus, and when to meditate will be helpful in guiding you to having the ultimate meditation experience.

Of course, one of the main tips for meditation is to find a time that's most convenient for you. If you feel like you have to fit in the session or may be interrupted, you're not going to be able to fully immerse yourself into the mindfulness you need for a successful meditation. Not only is it important to set aside a time when you won't be interrupted, but it's also good to have your own special place to meditate. It's best to pick a place where you're least likely to be disturbed, and is a place of comfort and relaxation. Although some of those more experienced with meditation are able to better tune out the outside noises and distractions, it's probably best for a beginner to choose a place of quiet and solace. Feel free to make this space your own. It's all about what will make you feel the most relaxed and comfortable so you can get all you can out of your meditations.

There are two simple tips to follow before you start your meditation. Do not eat right before meditation, and be sure to wear comfortable clothing. It's best not to eat at least an hour before meditation because you'll risk feeling groggy or sluggish while your food is digesting and you're trying to find a state of mindfulness. But also, you shouldn't be hungry either. You don't want the distraction of a growling stomach while you're trying to focus on your meditation. As far as clothing goes, be sure to wear what's comfortable to you, something that will allow you to relax and allow for fluid movement if you're going to be doing a meditation with movement.

Stretching and posture are things to consider before you start your meditation. You may or may not choose to stretch before your session. Some like to do a few yoga moves before meditation in order to warm up the muscles and also get in a more peaceful frame of mind that will ease you into a smooth transition for meditation. If you don't really feel the need for stretching, that's fine too. You may want to just take the time to focus on your posture before you meditate then. There is no right or wrong way to sit or hold your posture during meditation. Like everything else involved, just be sure that you are comfortable and will be able to sit comfortably for a period of time so that your mind doesn't stray to an achy back or a foot falling asleep. Of course there is the traditional way of sitting for meditation, which is sitting with your legs crossed. The most important thing to remember is to be comfortable with how you're sitting. Keep your body relaxed and keep the focus on your meditation. A comfortable and erect posture should be maintained throughout your meditation session. Feel free to add a cushion to support your back or any other part of your body you think may tire while you are meditating. This will take the strain off your body, and keep your mind free from the distraction of a possible sore or strained body part.

Let's cut to the chase: How do I sit?

There are two important principles that you need to bear in mind in setting up a suitable posture for meditation:

- **Your posture has to allow you to relax and to be comfortable**

- Your posture has to allow you to remain alert and aware

Both of these are vitally important. If you're uncomfortable you'll not be able to meditate because of discomfort. If you can't relax then you won't be able to enjoy the meditation practice and, just as importantly, you won't be able to let go of the underlying emotional conflicts that cause your physical tension.

From reading that, you might well think that it would be best to meditate lying down. Bad idea! If you're lying down your mind will be foggy at best, and you may well even fall asleep. If you've ever been to a yoga class that ends with shavasana (the corpse pose), where people lie on the floor and relax, you'll have noticed that about a third of the class is snoring within five minutes. Forget about meditating lying down. The best way to effectively combine relaxation AND awareness is a sitting posture. You don't have to sit cross-legged, or even sit on the floor.

We'll show you how to set up an effective posture in three positions: sitting in a chair, sitting astride a cushion or on a stool, and sitting cross-legged. All of these work: the important thing is to find one in which you will be comfortable.

Remember: you may think it looks really cool to sit cross-legged, but if you don't have the flexibility it takes to do that then you'll simply suffer! Make it easy on yourself. Choose a posture that is right for you.

Before we dive into different meditation postures, let's see the most important aspects of sitting properly:
1. Your spine should be upright, following its natural tendency to be slightly hollowed. You should neither be slumped nor have an exaggerated hollow in your lower spine.

2. Your spine should be relaxed.

3. Your shoulders should be relaxed, and slightly rolled back and down.

4. Your hands should be supported, either resting on a cushion or on your lap, so that your arms are relaxed.

5. Your head should be balanced evenly, with your chin slightly tucked in. The back of your neck should be relaxed, long, and open.

6. Your face should be relaxed, with your brow smooth, your eyes relaxed, your jaw relaxed, and your tongue relaxed and just touching the back of your teeth.

Take your position

Just as a tree needs to set down deep roots so it won't fall over as it grows, you need to find a comfortable position for the lower half of your body that you can sustain for 5 or 10 or 15 minutes — or even longer, if you wish. After several millennia of experimentation, the great meditators have come up with a handful of traditional postures that seem to work especially well. Different though they may appear from the outside, these postures have one thing in common: the pelvis tilts slightly forward, accentuating the natural curvature of the lower back.

The following poses are arranged more or less in order, from the easiest to the hardest to do, though ease all depends on your particular body and degree of flexibility. For example, some people take to the classical *lotus* position (whose name derives from its resemblance to the flower) like a duck to . . . well, to a lotus pond. Besides, the lotus, though difficult, has some definite advantages, and you can work up to it.

- **Sitting in a chair:** The trick to meditating in a chair is positioning your buttocks somewhat higher than your knees, which tilts your pelvis forward and helps keep your back straight. (See Figure 1.) Old-fashioned wooden kitchen chairs work better than the upholstered kind; experiment with a small cushion or foam wedge under your buttocks. Don't

slouch.

Figure 1: Position your buttocks a bit higher than your knees.

- **Kneeling (with or without a bench):** This technique was popular in ancient Egypt and in traditional Japan where it's called *seiza* (see Figure 2.). Kneeling can be — well, hard on your knees, unless you have proper support. Try placing a cushion under your buttocks and between your feet — or use a specially designed seiza bench, preferably one with a soft cushion between you and the wood. Otherwise, your bottom and other tender parts may fall asleep.

Figure 2: Kneeling can be hard on your knees, so try to add some cushioning.

- **Easy position:** Not recommended for extended periods of sitting because it's not very stable and doesn't support a straight spine. Simply sit on your cushion with your legs crossed in front of you tailor-fashion. (Believe it or not, tailors once sat this way!) Your knees don't have to touch the floor, but do keep your back as straight as you can.

You can stabilize the position by placing cushions under your knees; gradually decrease the height of the cushions as your hips become more flexible (which they naturally will over time).

When your knees touch the ground, you may be ready for Burmese or lotus position (see later bullets for these positions).

This pose can be a short-term alternative for people who can't manage the other positions in this list, can't kneel because of knee problems, or don't want to sit on a chair for some reason.

- **Burmese position:** This pose, shown in Figure 3, is used throughout Southeast Asia. This pose involves placing both calves and feet on the floor one in front of the other. Although less stable than the lotus series, it's much easier to negotiate, especially for beginners.

Figure 3: *The Burmese position is good for beginners.*

With all the cross-legged poses, first bend your leg at the knee, in line with your thigh, before rotating your thigh to the side. Otherwise, you risk injuring your knee, which is built to flex in only one direction, unlike the ball-and-socket joint of the hip, which can rotate through a full range of motion.

- **Quarter lotus:** Exactly like the half lotus, except that your foot rests on the calf of your opposite leg, rather than on the thigh.

- **Half lotus:** Easier to execute than the famous full lotus, and nearly as stable (see Figure 4). With your buttocks on a cushion, place one foot on the opposite thigh and the other foot on the floor beneath the opposite thigh. Be sure that both knees touch the floor and your spine doesn't tilt to one side. To distribute the pressure on your back and legs, remember to alternate legs from sitting to sitting, if you can — in other words, left leg on the thigh, right on the floor, then left on the floor and right on the thigh.

Figure 4: Both knees should touch the floor in the half lotus.

- **Full lotus:** Considered the Everest of sitting positions (see Figure 5). With your buttocks on a cushion, cross your left foot over your right thigh and your right foot over your left thigh. As with its more asymmetrical sibling, half lotus, it's best to alternate legs in order to distribute the pressure evenly.

Full lotus has been practiced throughout the world for many thousands of years. The most stable of all the poses, it should not be attempted unless you happen to be particularly flexible — and even then you should preparing by doing some stretches.

Figure 5: The full lotus is the "Everest" of sitting positions.

How long should each session last?

A question that may arise before beginning a meditation routine is how long you should meditate for. While the length of time one meditates for will vary from person to person, you may want to start out with shorter sessions and then gradually work your way up to longer meditations. You may find that your mind is only able to focus for a certain amount of time. If that's the case, then you'll want to choose shorter meditations. Once you get the hang of things, it will become easier to train your mind to meditate longer. The key is to be patient and allow yourself to work up to more prolonged meditations. It's also good to get into a routine for your meditation. Be consistent when you meditate. When a routine is established, you'll be able to devote ample time needed for your meditations. Typically, a mediation session of twenty to thirty minutes is sufficient. Listen to what your mind and body is telling you. It will know when you've reached your peak of mindfulness.

Breathing is an important component of meditation. Before you begin your session, you'll be mindful of your breathing, but eventually, as you get deeper into your meditation, the breathing will meld with your mindfulness and become a part of your mind and body. When you begin your meditation, focus on your breathing. This means be aware that you're breathing, know that you're breathing. Feel the rise and fall of your chest and the sensation of air filling your lungs and leaving as you exhale. Realize that breathing is a natural part of everything and is essential to your mindfulness. Develop your own breathing routine. Play around with what works and what doesn't, and you'll end up finding the perfect pattern of breathing that is conducive to your own mindfulness. Always remember that meditation is exercise for your brain, and like any type of exercise, your breathing is very important.

Another great tip to help with your meditation is how to deal with your emotions. We can't always have days where we can sit down and fall into our meditation without some sort of emotion whirling through our minds. And it's going to be difficult to settle into a meditation if your emotions aren't in check. Feelings such as anger, shame, and fear tend to resonate the strongest in our minds. One of the best ways to release these emotions for your meditation is to just go with them. Focus on what your body is feeling in regards to those emotions. For example, fear could be this feeling of a tight band around your chest. Focusing on that physical feeling and letting your mind work through it will help get your mind and body cleared of these emotions. Eventually you'll be free of these feelings that stand in the way of a clear meditation and you'll be focused on finding your mindfulness.

By using these tips and listening to your body and mind, you're well on your way to a successful meditation plan. Just remember to stick with it, and let your mindfulness fall into place.

Chapter 8
How Do I Build Upon A Meditation Habit? - Make It Long Term!

With all of the strategies provided on how to start meditating and how you can benefit from it, the next hurdle to overcome is how to stick with meditation over the long term. If you're not one to keep up with a goal or something you've started, it's important to find a meditation routine you're happy with and keep doing it. Meditation is not for those looking for instant gratification. It's a practice in patience and mindfulness, and its benefits will only be unlocked by the perseverant mind. This is why meditation, although being a great tool obtain relatively quick results (relaxation, increased focus, inner calmness), should be incorporated on your daily schedule over the long term in order to reap all its fruits.

So many have people have attested to the power of meditation and how it has played a vital role in changing their lives. Some have said it's the most powerful thing they've ever learned. Those types of statements alone should help influence you to keep up with your meditation habit. And one of the most amazing things about meditation is that it's really one of the simplest habits to build! It's not every day that one finds a healthy habit, one that will nourish the mind, body and soul. One of the things most people don't realize, however, is that having a meditation habit could be vital in improving or getting rid of other habits that aren't exactly beneficial to one's health.

Harness the power of Balance & Momentum

We have all been there: too much work, too little social life (or maybe even the other way around). Too much mental efforts, close to none physical training. Do you get where I'm going? Yes, I'm talking about balance.

Don't get me wrong: I do understand that balance can fade away on the short term in order to focus your energies exclusively on the task at hand. I've even once thought that one could live that way, but guess what? I was wrong. Although an unbalanced life can be tolerated for a while, it's no far from being a long term strategy. Especially if you care about living a long, happy, stress free life.

What does this all have to do with willpower, you may ask? Actually, a lot. Enduring self control can only be achieved if you are happy with your life. If you are not, then trying to –in top of everything else- get disciplined to do things you'd rather not do is a living hell on earth. It just can't be done on the long term.

Happiness is indeed one key aspect of highly disciplined people. Nevertheless, discipline and happiness are far from being the same thing: we all know somewhat happy people whose willpower is so weak that it makes me cry just to think about it. At the same time, you may even know some sad people who despite being unhappy manage to get their "to do lists" right on time.

But know what? The key is this: happiness without self-discipline and self discipline without happiness are both unsustainable over the long term. We need to be able to discipline ourselves to do things we'd rather not to right away in order to accomplish higher goals, while at the same time enjoy the road. Is that too much to ask? Of course not!

I known both you and I are trying to get a different kind of happiness from the "undisciplined happy person". You have picked up this book for a reason: you are willing to fight for the good things in life, not just take whatever it's thrown to you. That is why you need both, and in order to do that, why don't just make the road easier? It's all about setting the proper ground so that you can achieve all the things you know you can achieve.

I want you to find balance in your life, expanding in every possible way. Why should you? Simple: because there is a physical law that will help you out if you do. And if you don't, the same law will get back to you and attack you with all its power.

I'm talking about momentum. It works like this: as long as you are expanding, the subsequent improvements you set yourself up to will get easier. They will just flow. Think of it like riding a bicycle: at first it's hard, but once you get on going, movement replicates itself.

The same happens with self discipline. Once you get down to fight for what you want in life, each subsequent goal will get easier to achieve. Once you discipline yourself to exercise daily, taking up meditation will be almost effortless. Even more, once you've tackled exercising and meditation, eating the right foods will feel just natural. Further on, building a healthy lifestyle will get easier and easier.

At the same time, if your life is filled with crappy habits, they will replicate themselves. Just like a riding a bicycle, only that this time you'll be riding backwards. If you engage in behaviors that actually erode your willpower, what do you think will happen with your life in general? Each time you miss the gym you are not just "skipping one training session", you are actually destroying the self discipline you've worked so hard to develop! Once you do, you will be much more likely to skip the next meditation routine, and you'll probably end up eating garbage the next day. It's a physical law: there is no way around it. You just need to be aware of it so that you can use it in your favor!

Movement will replicate movement of the same kind. What kind that is it's up to you. Never forget this!

With our busy lives and hectic lifestyles, it's easy to make excuses as to why we don't have the time to keep up with a meditation routine. Maybe you can't make the time, perhaps you're too comfortable plopped on the couch in front of the television, or maybe you're buried in a mountain of paperwork for your job. Whatever the excuse may be, there's a simple solution: Make it easy so that you can't say no. While that may sound way too easy to be true, think about what its saying. When you start small and simple, you'll eventually work your way into keeping up with your habit, in this case meditation, and want to build upon your skills.

Starting out small is the key to incorporating a healthy habit into your lifestyle. With meditation, it's a matter of finding a time that works best for you, keeping your sessions short to begin with, and maintaining a schedule that keeps meditation in your daily routine. If you want to meditate, it's important that you do it on a regular basis. Before long, you'll realize that it's become second nature to get into your meditations.

When trying to maintain a meditation habit, it's important to be mindful of the negative thoughts that might be in your head. It's those negative thoughts that will try to sabotage the meditation habit that you've already tried to establish. A good example would be somebody who's trying to quit a smoking habit. Though they may be unaware of it, the stress or emotions of a long day or something that happened may take over their mind with negative emotions. When that happens, they will tend to make excuses for breaking their healthy habit. In the case of the smoker, they might tell themselves, what's one cigarette going to hurt? Although equating meditation with smoking is not in the same realm of healthiness, if you let your negative thoughts invade your mind, you'll find yourself putting off your meditation. Maybe it's only for a day. Then you'll find yourself making excuses for the next day and before you know it, you're not meditating at all anymore. These negative thoughts can be very tempting and powerful. But as you've come to realize, the power of meditation is even greater. Never underestimate the power your mind has over your will to do something, especially if that something is as beneficial as meditation. Leave those negative thoughts at the door and get in the good habit of not making excuses.

A great way to keep up with your meditation routine is to savor the habit. In other words, look forward to it and indulge in every moment you are in your state of mindfulness. Be aware of what you're experiencing when you meditate. By being aware of how the mediation is relaxing your mind, body, and spirit, you're going to want keep up with your sessions. As humans, we crave what makes us feel good, and as you indulge in the goodness that comes from meditation, you'll begin to realize that it should be a part of your daily healthy habits.

So what happens if you do fall off track with your meditation habit? It's important to remember to not be too hard on yourself. Things happen and sometimes we get caught up in the business of our lives. So have a plan when you falter with getting in your meditation. First, you need to make sure you re-start if you do falter. If it's been a few days, be sure to not let it go much longer and get back into your routine. Just be sure not to go past three days. Studies have found that missing one day is nothing too drastic, missing two days isn't exactly great, but you'll manage to recover, but after missing three days, the habit is pretty much shot. A great way to keep up with your meditation habit is get some accountability. Perhaps you will want to give yourself some sort of reward for keeping up with your sessions. Maybe at the end of the week you can treat yourself to dinner at your favorite restaurant. It's all about what motivates you to stick with your meditation habit. If you're having a bit of trouble with maintaining your habit, you can recruit a friend or family member to help hold you accountable. Perhaps for every day you miss a meditation, you must give this person a certain amount of money or have to do them a favor. Your motivation lies in not having to be held accountable and therefore you'll be sure to keep up with your meditations.

How Do Habits Form?

Habits (whether good or bad) form when a particular action (or set of actions) is performed repeatedly. They may feel unnatural to you at first, but with time, you get used to the actions and those actions become habit.

Habits are the mind's way of making sure that you can do certain things without thinking about them in an effort to become more productive. However, when bad habits form this way, they can turn your life into one of being less productive and efficient.

For instance, if you normally go without breakfast in the morning, you have become used to the habit of not eating in the morning.

However, if you start eating a slice of toast every morning before you go to work, you will find that, at first, it feels unusual to be doing this. If you stick with the routine, though, you will soon see that having this slice of toast has become a habit. This is because you do it every day.

The same can be said for someone who has never smoked before. When they smoke that first cigarette, it feels weird, but after repeated efforts, that person will soon make a habit of smoking (whether it is one a day or several an hour) – the habit will form.

The actual act of repeating something causes your brain to connect the situation with the action – so for instance, feeling stressful may cause you to smoke. You learn to associate smoking with stressful situations and vice versa.

If you really want to make a change, then try to focus on what is causing the habit and focus on the things you can do to improve that cause – don't focus on the habit itself.

An example here could be that you want to master the habit of eating more healthily. However, if you find that every time you become stressed or emotionally overwhelmed, you indulge in pizza and chocolate bars and, as a result, you feel comforted and happy; then trying to replace those things with things like eating more green vegetables and drinking vegetable juice will not fix the problem.

What you need to do is find a different way of calming yourself down when you become stressed or too emotional. In its simplicity, you need to generate the same feelings you get when eating pizza and chocolate, but you must do so in a way which is better for you, your health and your wellbeing.

When you can do this, you will soon find that you probably aren't eating as much junk food as you were before.

The bottom line when it comes to forming and keeping up with the meditation habit is simply just to do it. If you have to force yourself to keep up with it at the start, then so be it. Even if it takes simplifying your meditation habits to be able to fit it in everyday, you're still accomplishing and establishing a healthy habit of mindfulness. It's always important to keep your focus and maintain a schedule that works for you. Don't be discouraged if things don't seem to be working right away. As with all things meditation, patience is the key. Take your time, work yourself into a routine that fits your lifestyle, and you're sure to keep the healthy and mindful habit that is meditation.

Chapter 9
Tying Everything Into A Glorious Know - How Meditation Will Work For You

With so much information to absorb about the types of meditation, what sort of meditation will be right for you, and figuring out how to maintain a steady meditation habit, it's normal to be overwhelmed. It can be a lot to take it, but it doesn't have to be a complicated process. The path to finding your road to mindfulness will lead to an awakening of your mind, body, and spirit. With the patience and the knowledge, you're bound to find what works best for you.

Remember that meditation is surrender. It's about surrendering your stresses, your worries, your fears, and all of the negative emotions that are holding you back from living your life fully. When you meditate, you're nourishing your mind. And when your mind is nourished, the rest of your body will fall into sync. If you're more of the religious or spiritual type, you can think of meditation as fuel for your spiritual growth. And since meditation has been around since ancient times, it has quite an impressive track record when it comes to changing lives.

If you tend to lead a stressful lifestyle, you've already learned about what that kind of thing can do to your body. Stress is an everyday part of life, but it doesn't have to be something that consumes you and wreaks havoc on your mind and body. Think of that stress as a plague. Not only a physical plague, but a mental one as well. The longer you let it run its course through your body, the worse off you're going to be. Meditation is a proven way to battle this stress and help eliminate it from your life. Through mediation, you'll gain a mindfulness that will help you put a healthy distance between you and that stress that tends to take over your thoughts. Through meditation, you'll be able to see things clearly, as if you're seeing that distance you've put between you and the stress, and will be able to successfully let it go.

You may be wondering how mediation is going to be different from the other things and techniques you may have tried in order to achieve a feeling of balance in your life. How is meditation set apart from just simply relaxing, thinking, concentration, or practicing self-hypnosis? Meditation is different from these other forms of mental exercise because it's truly relaxing to the brain. Not only does it relax us, but it infuses our minds and bodies with optimism, peace, and joy. Not only that, but it can transform us from being the typical over-stressed and tired human, to more deeply beautiful and enriched persons. Mindfulness is a powerful thing. And being able to use that mindfulness to enhance and better one's life is a truly humbling experience.

Don't forget to remember what the main purposes of meditation are. If you're seeking out a more relaxed state of mind, then you already have your reason and incentive for deciding to incorporate mindfulness into your everyday life. Meditation is getting your mind and body into a state of silence. Nothing else exists aside from your focus on the calm and serene. It's in this silence that we can look inside ourselves with an introspect that has no pride, no guilt, no fears, and no stress. Through mediation, we can extend far beyond mere relaxation. We can experience an awareness where we are not weighed down by the thoughts of anxiety, stress, and negative emotion plaguing our conscious minds. By being in the presence of our own minds, we are able to experience our true nature and find a peace and focus we may never have known existed within us had we continued down a path absent of mindfulness.

Embrace meditation as your own. Don't think of it as something you have to do or are forced to partake in. You'll be missing the whole point of finding your mindfulness and focus for a clearer and more relaxed mind. You cannot force meditation. Let it come to you. Once again, patience is the essence of allowing yourself to be fully immersed in the innumerable benefits meditation can bestow upon you. Meditation is not something you can buy or sell. It's not something you can hope to learn through shortcuts or only going through the motions and not fully committing yourself to mindfulness. It's also important to dispel all of the myths you may have about meditation from your mind before starting your own routine. If you go into it thinking you're going to have some sort of miraculous experience that is nothing short of a spiritual miracle, then you're seeking out meditation for all the wrong reasons. Keep it simple and eventually you'll get to where you need to be with your focus and mindfulness.

Above all else, when making the decision to start meditating, know that you are well on your way to finding your inner beauty and peace. The ability to love oneself as well as other fellow human beings is one of the most beautiful qualities we have as human beings. With meditation, we have the ability and capacity to trigger this trait more deeply and spiritually. When we are able to find our inner happiness   and beauty from within as an individual, we are able to take that and practice it with others. Through meditation and your mindfulness, you'll see the world in a different way. It will be a more positive, inviting, beautiful, and stress free place. This comes from being aware of your inner focus and being able to channel that peace and apply it to your everyday life. When we are in a calmer, more peaceful, and more focused state of mind, we are able to have a positive influence on those around us. And because the key to all of this positivity comes from incorporating meditation into our lives, there's no question that it will change your life for the better.

Thank you for reading this book on Zen Buddhism.

I realize, some of the more critical readers out there might try to argue that not all of these tips were derived from the Zen Buddhist scriptures—I didn't, for example, talk about Japanese Zen gardens or go into too much detail about what Bodhidharma, the father of Zen Buddhism, taught.

That was deliberate. This book is quite clear in its intention: I wanted to provide you with daily tools that help integrate what Zen masters of old taught us, that we can functionally integrate into our lives. If you want to read about the history and culture of Zen lifestyles, there are thousands of books out there in every languages that can help you do that. I recommend you visit your library or Amazon and find some.

Rather than delve into the historical details, I wanted to write a practical guide that you could take home with you, read on the bus or in bed—*alone*, preferably—and hold up in juxtaposition with your own life. Think about this, now: can you honestly say that you can simplify your life? Have you broken down your own mental barriers? Are you terrified of being alone? Do you keep sentimental reminders from 20 years ago in your basement, because you're afraid to let go of the past?

It's very easy to overcome these things, physically. Throw out the trash. Sit alone in a room. Meditation is—let's be honest for a moment here—literally just the act of doing *nothing*. The easiest things we can do are the things we never seem to want to do. It's painfully ironic.

But what I want to help you figure out is that you can overcome these distinctly modern problems. We need not fear loneliness, for we were born into it and will die in it. We are plainly vain to focus on what others think of us, and place it before our own sense of self-importance. We can afford to take some time to meditate, or pull our cars over and release our emotions if the moment strikes us. We should not feel confined by the contrivances of contemporary society.

I'd like to end on a story, the story of when the Buddha achieved enlightenment. It was written several hundred years after Buddha Gautama's death, but is credited in Mahayana Buddhism—and, as a result, Zen Buddhism—as a reasonably accurate quote. Regardless of its accuracy, it sums up the core of Zen belief perfectly:

> "I consider the positions of kings and rulers as that of dust motes. I observe treasures of gold and gems as so many bricks and pebbles. I look upon the finest silken robes as tattered rags. I see myriad worlds of the universe as small seeds of fruit, and the greatest lake in India as a drop of oil on my foot. I perceive the teachings of the world to be the illusion of magicians. I discern the highest conception of emancipation as a golden brocade in a dream, and view the holy path of the illuminated ones as flowers appearing in one's eyes. I see meditation as a pillar of a mountain, Nirvana as a nightmare of daytime. I look upon the judgment of right and wrong as the serpentine dance of a dragon, and the rise and fall of beliefs as but traces left by the four seasons."

To your success,

Dominique Francon

Preview Of "Buddhism For Beginners! - The Ultimate Guide To Incorporate Buddhism Into Your Life – A Buddhism Approach For More Energy, Focus, And Inner Peace"

Introduction
Buddhism CAN Change Your Life, Did You Know That?

There's a common misconception that Buddhism is somehow *harder* than Christianity. Think about Christianity: it's easy, right? So, if someone alien were to ask you to describe Christianity, what would you say to them?

Would you describe the imagery of Catholicism, the relevance of the Virgin Mary and emphasis on confessions before God?

Would you talk about the evolution of Protestantism, starting with Martin Luther and how Christianity aims to guide people to be more like Jesus Christ in their actions?

Would you start even further back, all the way back to the writing of the Bible? Before or after the Old Testament? To be truly accurate you'd have to include Abraham and Isaac, and explain most of Judaism while you're at it.

Would you talk about Episcopalians? The United Church? The Westboro Baptist Church? Anglicans? Jehovah's Witnesses? Gospel choirs? The Crusades?

In other words: where do you start, and where do you end?

The fact is that all religions are extremely complex, and Buddhism is no different. Buddhism can't be boiled down into a single phrase: "It's about achieving a Zen understanding of the world, and feeling at peace"—that only begins to describe some of the complexities of a proper Buddhist lifestyle.

But that doesn't mean that Buddhism is difficult to learn. That's why I'm writing this book. I want to help you understand Buddhism from a ground-level, from a totally introductory standpoint, so you can take from it what you'd like. This book isn't meant to convert you to any religion (everyone knows that, as far as conversions go, Buddhists are probably the least likely), but it instead aims to guide you towards understanding what has been the dominant eastern religion for over 2,000 years.

Buddhism isn't alone in this respect—there's divergence with Hinduism, Taoism and Japanese Zen philosophy. They're roughly similar in the way that Judaism, Christianity and Islam are similar—which they are, actually, because they're all based on the same original stories of Abraham and Isaac, and all deify a supremely powerful being, just in different forms. (The Jewish God was later split into three—the Father, the Son and the Holy Spirit—and Muslims interpreted Him as Allah—but He's actually the same guy in every instance.)

Similarly, there are a myriad forms of Buddhism: Mahayana, Theravada, Cheontae, Zen, Nichiren, Shingon... the list goes on.

And, in fact, Buddhism shares many moral and ethical similarities with Christianity and Judaism. Pretty much every religion, at the end of the day, advocates being a good person, doing good deeds, not committing crimes and helping others. In all respects, education and wisdom is revered over all. Buddhism is much the same. Consider this quote: "Drop by drop is the water pot filled. Likewise, the wise man, gathering it little by little, fills himself with good."

Literally any religious figure could have gotten away with saying that. But you know what? It was the original Buddha.

In order to get the most out of Buddhism and help your day-to-day life, we're not going to focus on the little differences between Buddhism sects. I'll introduce them to you in the first two chapters, along with what Buddhism teaches and what the religion is all about *in a nutshell*, because it's important to grasp the key concepts if you want to understand how to implement it in your life. Then we'll discuss what Buddhism teaches us on a practical level, dealing with subjects such as living in the present moment, the power of meditation and yoga (which are, actually, more similar than you might believe) and how the age-old concept of karma—including rebirth and how good deeds beget happiness—can help guide us through everyday life, even if we don't believe it literally.

The fact is, like all religions, it is not only difficult but extremely dangerous to follow it 100 percent. We've come to a point as a global society—with the ease of access to information that the internet has provided, and now that we can hear so many different viewpoints, philosophies and religious beliefs—that individualizing is becoming important and popular. There's a reason that every religion is seeing smaller and smaller numbers each year. Churches report lower attendance records, and most Jews identify more with the secular Woody Allen and Jerry Seinfeld than the ancient wise man Rabbi Hillel.

And more than that, we're learning that it's not a crime to dip into multiple religions. You can turn the other cheek like Jesus says, and also celebrate Passover with your Jewish friends. We've successfully convinced ourselves that, as long as we are true and decent people, which God we believe in matters less than how we live our lives.

And you know what? That's what Buddhism teaches us.

Buddhism is a *nontheistic* religion. That means Buddhists don't believe in a One Almighty God. Buddhists instead try to find inner peace, within themselves, not relying on an outside being to teach them. It is a religion based on self-importance, self-respect and, perhaps most importantly, self-discipline. That makes it easy to adopt certain Buddhist practices into our daily lives. Heck, we do it already, all the time—think of yoga, or mantras, or we repeat to ourselves, or the belief in good and bad karma, or meditation. These are all phrases and acts adopted from Buddhism, which have seeped into our everyday lives and our everyday vocabulary.

When you think of it that way, Buddhism isn't so foreign.

But wait, you might be saying. Back up a second. If there's no God, then who are all those statues of? Who's the big fat laughing guy, and the snarling big-eared one? And who was the original Buddha, if not a God?

And you know what? I'm going to answer all those questions in the upcoming chapters. There are too many questions. Questions are crucial in Buddhism—it's a good thing to ask them. Hopefully, I'll be able to answer as many as I can.

The fact is that Buddhism, as we know it today, has been around for over 2,000 years and has been the foundation of dozens of civilizations—some successful, some now extinct. Buddhist structures, statues and temples are some of the most historically enduring and spiritually meaningful monuments in the world: think of Cambodia's mighty Ankor Wat, a massive temple complex over 1,000-years-old; Borobudur, a magnificent ancient stone pyramid in central Java, Indonesia, that welcome a gorgeous sunrise every morning; the Hill Temple, nestled between vibrant green trees and overlooking the ancient city of Kyoto, Japan; Thailand's Wat Pho, with a famously luxurious-looking reclining Buddha, said to be the birthplace of Thai massage; and South

Korea's colorful temples, like Guinsa and Haeinsa, filled with chanting monks and towering stone pagodas.

Buddhism is no joke. It's not a small belief, and it's historically older than our Biblical realities, dating back to the 5th and 6th century BC. There's no excuse to be ignorant of what the eastern half of the world believes, and there's no reason we can't learn from it.

So, for now, put your mind at ease. Put on some soft, meditative music. And let's get started.

Chapter 1
Who the First Buddha Was & What He Taught

There once was a man, around 2,600 years ago, who was born in northern India, in the foothills of the Himalayan mountains, which is now part of southern Nepal. His name was Siddhartha Gautama. Gautama was born into royalty as an opulent young aristocratic prince, with a life surrounded by comfort and luxury.

But Gautama had a problem: he wasn't very happy. It's the age-old story of "money can't buy you happiness," and it doesn't buy Gautama any joy at all. He finds himself confused, restless and constantly questioning of everything. He had a philosophical mind.

So, discouraged by his lifestyle, Gautama left his palace at the age of 29 in search of greater meaning in the world. This was the first time he had left home and witnessed the outside world. He saw the problems of the world for the first time: the sick, the old, the suffering. The naïve prince was eager to learn more about these real-world problems. He started going on more trips outside the palace to interact with people more people who were diseased, vain and dying. These problems depressed him immensely, and he decided to change his lifestyle completely.

He became an ascetic—one who abstains from mortal pleasures. He threw himself into a world devoid of expensive belongings and material wealth, and began begging for alms, pure charity, in the street. His goal was humility.

Eventually someone spotted and recognized him (as a prince, you'd think it wouldn't take too long) and tried to bring him back to the world of royalty. He denied this offer, too, and instead changed course: he began seeking out every great philosophical mind of his time, looking for answers to his problems of happiness.

He went to practice yogic meditation with the masters, and excelled at it to the point of being offered to succeed the masters as a permanent teacher, but Gautama denied this offer, too. He tried a different sort of yoga under a different teacher, and attained a high plateau of meditative consciousness—again, impressed with his determination, the then-master asked him to stay. But Gautama still wasn't satisfied.

He then turned to self-mortification: a deeper kind of humility. He deprived himself of all worldly luxuries, including food. Allegedly eating only a single leaf or nut per day, he nearly starved himself to death. He wanted no part of any world that would continue to offer him luxuries of any sort, including status as a "master" or "king". The very thought of hierarchy put a bad taste in his mouth.

By now he was 35-years-old, and found himself sitting beneath what has today become famous as the Bodhi Tree, now in Bodh Gaya, India, in the distant groves near the Neranjara riverbanks. He fell, nearly unconscious due to starvation, and promised himself he wouldn't wake up until he'd found enlightenment. He then fell into a deep meditative state, and found a previously unimaginable state of clear and thorough consciousness. He began thinking about the world, the universe, the nature of life.

This took 49 days, so the legend goes.

From that point on, he was known as the Buddha—or, later, once more Buddhas start popping up throughout history (and yes, there are at least 28 more; but no, we won't get into all of them in as much detail), he became known as the Supreme Buddha. "Buddha" means, simply, "Awakened One" or "Enlightened One," so the title fits.

What Did He Learn?

It's complicated, even impossible, to know exactly what he thought that night he underwent enlightenment. Certainly, at the very least, he shoved aside ascetism and self-mortification, along with self-indulgence at every level. He essentially created Buddhism as we know it today, and though what exactly that means can be vague, he does provide some helpful guides, which are known as dharma.

He wrote down his newfound doctrine based on what we know as "The Four Noble Truths", through which followers of Buddhism can reach Nirvana. Nirvana is the end goal in Buddhism: it is a state of awesome freedom, total ease of mind and mental mastery. To translate it into religious terms, it's heaven on earth. Anyone can reach a state of mental nirvana through dedication to Buddhism and following the teachings of Gautama.

To be in a state of nirvana means to ignore greed, selfishness, anger and other distracting emotions. It is, in a word, to be emotionally *above* the rest of the world. It sounds a bit haughty, but the idea is this completely carelessness about oneself, a delicate balance between being self-centered and not being egocentric. Nirvana means being altruistic and kind, understanding selflessness enough to know how small you are in the universe, and being okay with that.

According to one story, immediately after waking up from his Enlightenment, the Buddha wasn't sure if he should teach others his dharma. He wasn't sure everyone could handle it: after all, humans are afflicted by greed and ignorance all the time, which is why he had to go through this six-year meditative process to figure it out at all. Buddha told his problem to a friend, who convinced him that at least some people will grasp his meaning. Buddha agreed to have faith, and so the dharma was born into public.

What Does He Teach?

We're going to break down Buddhism really simply for you now, just because, well, this is an eBook, and we have a lot of other topics to touch on. So excuse me as I skip some of the details and sections like the Five Skandhas and Six Realms, which basically explain how to view life, and instead focus on what the Supreme Buddha wants *you* to learn.

The Four Noble Truths

There are four realities to face when you look at the world. The Four Noble Truths were what the Supreme Buddha first taught in his very first sermons to the public, so this is very Buddha-101 appropriate.

The first truth is that *there is suffering in the world*. We may know this phrase as, "Shit happens." Basically, life can be difficult—loved ones get hit by cars, our pets get cancer, we get fired, babies die in the womb, an African child just died as you read this sentence, schools get shot up; even if you avoid all of this, in the best-case scenario, you're going to die one day. Basically, there is pain, strife and difficulty. This is a truth of the world, and the first one we must face in order to achieve enlightenment: even if our own particular lives are mostly okay (i.e. none of the above apply, save for the death bit), the world is a harsh and brutal place. The First Noble Truth tells us that we must mentally face this head-on: think about it. Believe in it. Confront it.

The second truth defines this suffering: *every suffering has a cause*. There are a few causes. One is a craving for something: for respect, for power, for control, for material happiness. The other reasons we suffer are because we are trying to define ourselves as something we are not, or do not want to be; for example, if we're sad but want to be happy, we are trying to redefine ourselves in that moment. We try to unite with experiences in the way that we want to be constantly connected to the outside world, have a past, present and future life, and be successful. Or else we crave the opposite: to not feel sad when we don't want to, or to escape from painful emotions.

The Third Noble Truth is that *your suffering can end*. It is possible, in other words, to remove ourselves from our problems. We can rethink our lives, and redefine our personalities. Once we realize how loosely tied we are to our personalities, we can work on new ones. We don't need to pretend to fit in when we don't. We don't need to impress people we don't get alone with. We could be simpler than that, and focus on affirming ourselves to ourselves alone. We need to remove the cravings from the Second Noble Truth and focus on our real needs.

The fourth and final Noble Truth is *how to end the suffering*. It's a subtle wording difference from number three, but a significant one: while three tells us *that we can* end our suffering, four begins to tell us *how*. The answer is, basically, mindful meditation; in a longer answer, the path to happiness involves what's called **The Eightfold Path**.

The Eightfold Path

The Eightfold Path is crucial to every Buddhist practice, and comprises the Fourth Noble Truth in its entirety. It is the path to enlightenment, true understanding and personal happiness.

At the risk of turning this chapter into an extremely dense introduction, I'm going to go over the Eightfold Path very quickly, in point-form, so as to not overload you all at once.

The Noble Eightfold Path is divided into eight ways to act correctly. They're called the Rights. So remember that when you read Right here, it means Right as in Objectively Correct.

The eight Rights are divided into three sub-sections, including Wisdom, Ethical Conduct and Concentration.

The two filed under *Wisdom* describe a proper Buddhist mental state:

1. **Right View** – Sometimes called "Right Perspective" or "Right Outlook", this can be summed up as the proper way of looking at the nature of things, the way the world exists in its natural form, which can adopt an almost scientific perspective: physics, chemistry and biology all dictate our world.

2. **Right Thought** – Thinking good thoughts will give you a good life. To achieve this you must mentally renounce material goods and think instead about what matters: good deeds, peacekeeping, charity and being kind towards others.

The three steps under *Ethical Conduct* progress this lifestyle into reality:

3. **Right Speech** – So, you've got those good thoughts in your head? Speak them. No lying, no wasteful chitchat, no insults.

4. **Right Action** – Talk is cheap—do good deeds. Don't kill, steal or rape.

5. **Right Livelihood** – Don't make your job an evil one. Don't create weapons, don't trade slaves, don't sell drugs, don't kill people. According to Buddha, the "business of meat" is also a no-no; sorry, butchers.

The last three, under *Concentration*, might be the hardest to achieve:

6. **Right Effort** – This describes preventative measures. If you're leading a true Buddhist life, you will need effort to actively subdue your material and worldly urges. Be mindful of the good that has no yet risen within yourself, and abstain from the evil.

7. **Right Mindfulness** – Also translated as "Right Memory", to be mindful of something means you're keeping it in mind. You should be constantly aware of every part of your body, in tune with your health and mental state, to continue your other Right ways.

8. **Right Concentration** – Also known as "Right Meditation", this simply defines an ideal meditative state: one aloof from the world, purely tranquil and absorbed by your mental cleanness.

Phew! That about sums it up. Thanks for hanging in there. I know this stuff can get a little dense at times, but, as the Noble Eightfold Path shows, it's actually pretty natural. It's the same basic morality as suggested by Abrahamic religions: think good thoughts, do good deeds, and stay that way.

The big departures in Buddhism come in the specific logic of the religion. The description of the mind and body is different from the Christian conception of the soul. Nirvana is different from heaven. But only in logical terms.

If looked at abstractly, from a bit far away, you'll find that the first of the Four Noble Truths—that there is suffering in the world—is an issue debated and tackled by every major religion in the world. Others might simply chalk it up to the old phrase, "God works in mysterious ways." The big change in Buddhism is that it tries to define that problem and, instead of promoting belief in God or Jesus to save you from such dangers and bring you to heaven, the Supreme Buddha suggests believing in yourself and overcoming these worldly problems while you're still on Earth.

This is by no means a comprehensive analysis—we still haven't gotten to karma, rebirth or the thousands of other little details that create Buddhism. But we'll get there soon.

For now, and in the next chapter, we're going to look at a few variations of Buddhism, and how it's affected the world as we know it.

To check out the rest of "Buddhism For Beginners! - The Ultimate Guide To Incorporate Buddhism Into Your Life – A Buddhism Approach For More Energy, Focus, And Inner Peace", **click here or go to Amazon and look for it right now!**

Ps: You'll find many more books like these under my name, Dominique Francon.
Don't miss them! <u>Here's a short list:</u>

- Buddhism For Beginners
- Meditation For Beginners
- Reiki For Beginners
- Yoga For Beginners

- Running Will Make You FIT
- Cycling HIIT Training

- Paleo Recipe Cookbooks
- Much, much more!

About the Author

Dominique Francon is a significant health connoisseur devoted to helping others get healthy all around the world.

From a very young age, Francon understood the value and potential of leading a healthy lifestyle. And because of her genuine appreciation and enthusiasm for all things health-related, she has dedicated a great deal of time and effort to researching the best of what fitness, nutritional diets and overall wellbeing programs have to offer.

In the beginning, Francon focused on working with people in various gym and sports club settings. Before long she became exceedingly in tune with the health and fitness solutions that had the best results for her clients' issues and goals. But after years of accumulating one health expertise following another, Francon decided she wanted to reach out to even more individuals.

She wanted to help people on a bigger scale. For this reason she resolved to share her extensive knowledge with people through writing and publishing books pertaining to her vast health-related know-how. Currently she has authored books on such cutting-edge topics as paleo cooking, Zen, Yoga, running and cycling.

Francon has a real passion for all the subjects she writes about and she takes the job seriously. She knows self-development is, for a lot of people, as significant as it is for her. But she also knows how tough it is to change one's lifestyle. With this in mind, her aim while writing is to make the concepts and instructions as helpful and accessible to her readers as possible. After all, for her the end objective is improving the lives of others.

CPSIA information can be obtained at www.ICGtesting.com
Printed in the USA
LVOW07s0548280715

447817LV00025B/799/P

9 781502 349194